ROBOTS
THINKING AND LEARNING

www.worldbook.com

Co-published by agreement between Shi Tu Hui and World Book, Inc.

Shi Tu Hui
Room 1807, Block 1,
#3 West Dawang Road
Chaoyang District, Beijing 100025
P.R. China

World Book, Inc.
180 North LaSalle Street
Suite 900
Chicago, Illinois 60601
USA

© 2026. All rights reserved. This volume may not be reproduced in whole or in part in any form without prior written permission from the publisher.

WORLD BOOK and the GLOBE DEVICE are registered trademarks or trademarks of World Book, Inc.

Library of Congress Control Number: 2025938161

Robots
ISBN: 978-0-7166-5814-6 (set, hard cover)

Robots Thinking and Learning
ISBN: 978-0-7166-5817-7 (hard cover)

Also available as:
ISBN: 978-0-7166-5827-6 (soft cover)
ISBN: 978-0-7166-5837-5 (e-book)

WORLD BOOK STAFF

Writer: William D. Adams

Editorial

Vice President
Tom Evans

Senior Manager, New Content
Jeff De La Rosa

Associate Manager, New Content
William D. Adams

Content Creator
Elizabeth Huyck

Proofreader
Nathalie Strassheim

Graphics and Design

*Senior Visual
Communications Designer*
Melanie Bender

Photo Editor
Rosalia Bledsoe

ACKNOWLEDGMENTS

Cover: © 35lab/Shutterstock; © Elena11/Shutterstock; © Boston Dynamics; © Feel Good Luck/Shutterstock

4-5 © Tinnaporn Sathapornnanont, Shutterstock; © Sony Corporation
6-7 © Omer Faruk Boyaci, Shutterstock; Smithsonian Institution
8-9 Portrait of Jacques de Vaucanson (1784), oil on canvas by Joseph Boze; Academy of Sciences/Institut de France (Paris); Public Domain
10-11 © Kazuhiro Nogi, Getty Images
12-13 © Jeremy Sutton-Hibbert, Alamy Images
14-15 © Kazuhiro Nogi, Getty Images; Humanrobo (licensed under CC BY-SA 3.0)
16-17 © Rodrigo Reyes Marin/AFLO/Alamy Images
18-19 © RoboCup Federation
20-21 Peter Schulz (licensed under CC BY-SA 4.0); © RoboCup Federation
22-23 © SoftBank Robotics
24-25 © Francois Nel, Getty Images; © Philip Lange, Shutterstock
27-29 © Georgia Institute of Technology
30-31 © Bettmann/Getty Images; © Jack Taylor, Getty Images
32-33 © Boston Dynamics
34-35 © Anki
36-37 © Matthew Fearn, PA Images/Getty Images; © Innvo Labs Corporation
38-39 © Sony Corporation
40-41 © Good Moments/Shutterstock; © Ned Snowman, Shutterstock
42-43 © Ozobot & Evollve; © Sphero
44-45 © Wonder Workshop, Inc; © Alesia Kan, Shutterstock
46-47 © Ground Picture/Shutterstock

Contents

- **4** Introduction
- **6** How Smart Are Robots?
- **8** A Robot's Brain
- **10** Autonomy
- **12** Artificial Intelligence
- **14** Bottom-Up Robotics
- **16** HELLO, MY NAME IS: Elmer and Elsie
- **18** Uses of Bottom-Up Robotics
- **20** Top-Down Robotics
- **22** Machine Learning
- **24** Supervised Learning
- **26** Unsupervised Learning
- **28** Learning Like Us: Neural Networks
- **30** Learning from Demonstration
- **32** HELLO, MY NAME IS: Spot
- **34** ROBOT CHALLENGE: Is Learning Worth the Effort?
- **36** Learning Through Play
- **38** Learning Together
- **40** Robot Rights
- **42** Robot Responsibilities
- **44** Living with Smarter Robots
- **46** Hands-On Robotics
- **48** Glossary and Index

Terms defined in the glossary are in type **that looks like this** on their first appearance on any spread (two facing pages).

introduction

We humans are great learners. By attending school, absorbing lessons and advice from elders and peers, and even through play, we take in and organize huge amounts of information about the world around us.

Most traditional robots, on the other hand, aren't great learners. They are carefully programmed to perform specific tasks. If something unexpected happens that the 'bot isn't programmed to deal with, it will probably botch the job and require human help. It can be reprogrammed to perform a different task, but this isn't learning—it's like wiping a slate clean and starting over again. Robots that don't learn mostly work in **structured environments** where they will not be disrupted by unexpected events.

But with new advances in computing and **artificial intelligence,** engineers and programmers are designing new robots that can cope in **unstructured environments.** These learning robots will be at home in our homes and workplaces and on our streets.

In this book, you will read how robots process and react to their environments. You will learn how some robots learn. You will also get to meet some learning robots.

"DOES NOT COMPUTE!"
Robots are great at repetitive tasks, but without special programming they have a tough time learning new things.

How Smart Are Robots?

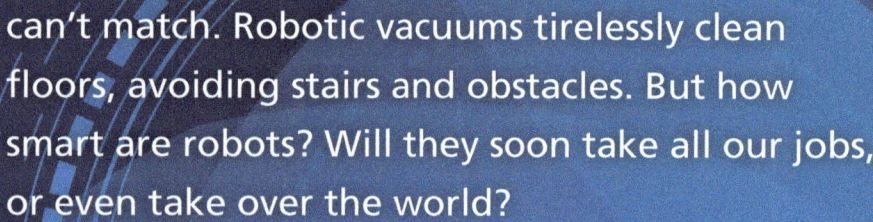

Robots are often really good at their jobs. **Industrial robots** can assemble parts with a speed and precision that humans can't match. Robotic vacuums tirelessly clean floors, avoiding stairs and obstacles. But how smart are robots? Will they soon take all our jobs, or even take over the world?

Good news: You're smarter than any robot that's ever been made! That's because people, unlike robots, possess what's called general intelligence. A robot or computer might do one task with blinding speed, but they would be useless if asked to do something else. A single person, however, can perform all kinds of tasks and calculations, even if not as quickly as a robot or computer. Even the most advanced robots and computer programs don't have general intelligence.

One-trick pony
Robots lack the intelligence—and often, the physical ability—to master new tasks, as people can. This robotic lawnmower is great at trimming grass. But you would not ask it to drive your car.

A Robot's Brain

Every robot has a computer that guides its actions. Its **hardware** is selected to best suit its job. Robots have computer programs, or **software,** that instruct them on what goals to achieve and how to achieve them. Almost all robots have software that can be reprogrammed to work toward different goals.

Sensors gather information about the robot's environment. The computer processes this information and decides how the robot should respond based on the program stored in its memory. It then directs the **actuators** and **effectors** of the robot to carry out this response. This cycle is called *sense-plan-act.*

A robot's program may be extremely complex to prepare it for as many situations as possible, especially if it works in an **unstructured environment.** Advances in **artificial intelligence** are also helping robots to become more adaptable.

Thinking clearly
The **android** Sophia's see-through head reveals the hardware it uses to hold basic conversations and control the motors in its face.

Autonomy

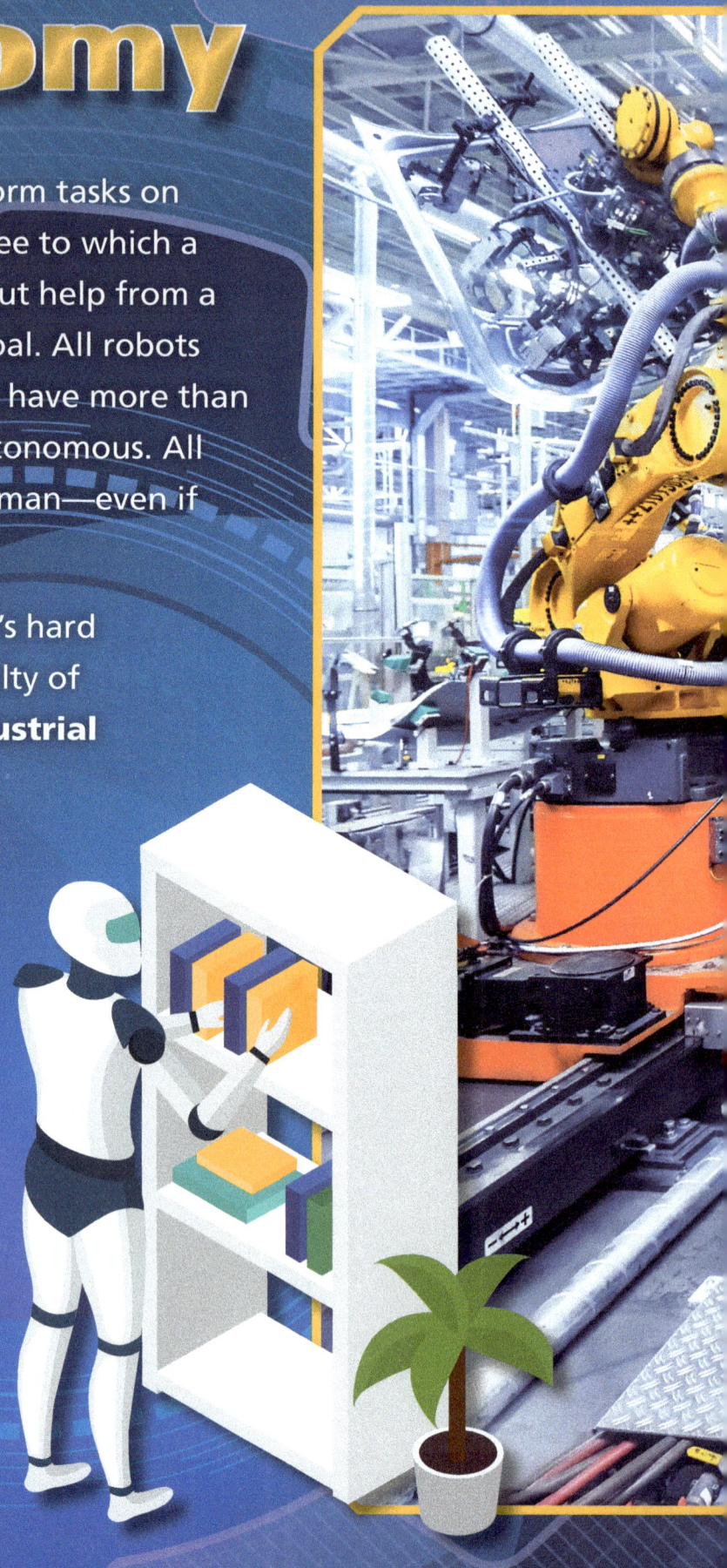

To be useful, a robot must perform tasks on its own. **Autonomy** is the degree to which a robot can make decisions without help from a human operator to achieve a goal. All robots have some autonomy, but some have more than others. And no robot is fully autonomous. All must have some help from a human—even if just in picking the robot's task.

Although autonomy is useful, it's hard to program. To avoid the difficulty of programming autonomous **industrial robots,** engineers often place them in carefully designed **structured environments** that limit unexpected events. In **unstructured environments,** unexpected events happen all the time. It is impossible to program for everything a robot might encounter. But artificial intelligence is helping robots to learn from experience and know when to ask a human for help.

[10]

In their own little world
Most industrial robots are kept in highly controlled, structured environments to limit the autonomy they need to do their jobs.

Artificial Intelligence

The most **autonomous** robots and computers often make use of a type of programming known as **artificial intelligence.** Artificial intelligence (AI) is the ability of a computer system to process information in a manner similar to human thought or to exhibit humanlike behavior.

People used to think of AI as science fiction, or always just beyond the horizon. But today AI is all around us. It isn't as advanced as in the movies, but it is improving rapidly. AI has already changed many fields, including science, economics, and marketing.

How do you make an artificially intelligent robot? Programming strategies fall into two camps: bottom-up, or behavior-based, robotics and top-down, or traditional, robotics.

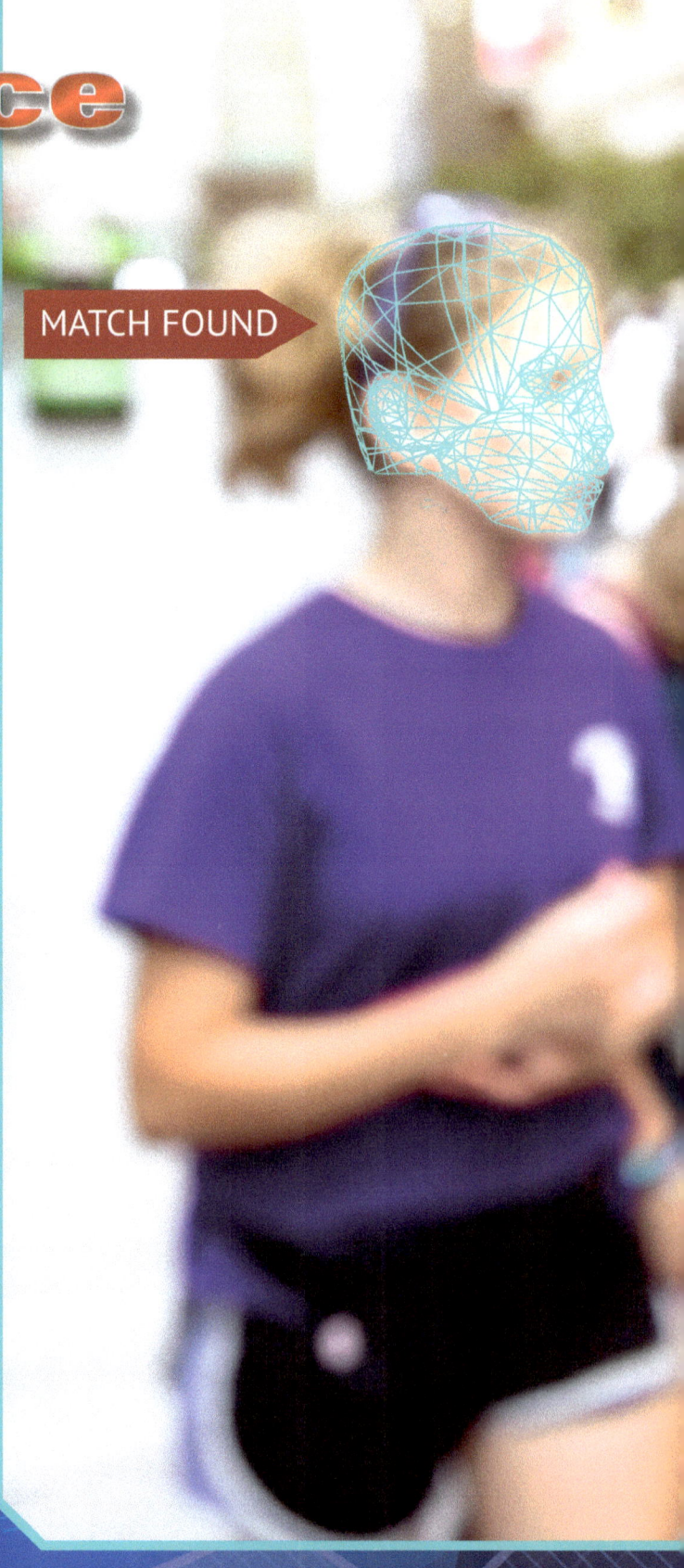

MATCH FOUND

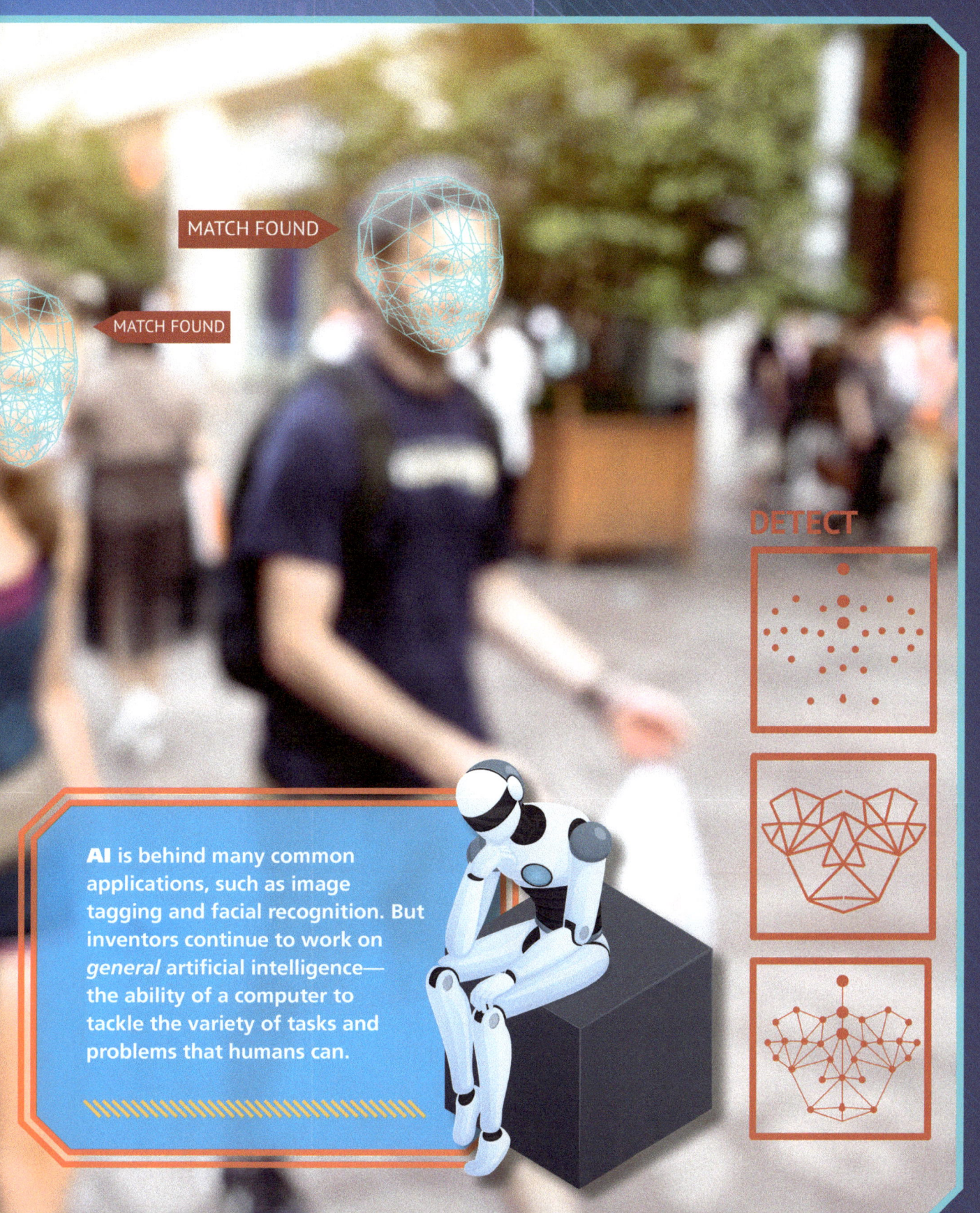

MATCH FOUND

MATCH FOUND

DETECT

AI is behind many common applications, such as image tagging and facial recognition. But inventors continue to work on *general* artificial intelligence—the ability of a computer to tackle the variety of tasks and problems that humans can.

Bottom-Up Robotics

Think about an insect: It's small and doesn't have much of a brain, but it's able to survive in all kinds of environments. A bug's body systems are only loosely connected. Its brain isn't as important to it as yours is to you. Many insects can survive for days without a head!

The experimental robot Genghis worked—and looked—much like an insect.

Some programmers believe imitating these simple animals is the best way to build intelligent, **autonomous** robots. Groups of simple, self-contained instruction modules could combine to create robots that perform a wide variety of tasks. This is called emergent behavior. Such robots would also be more resistant to damage or hacking. A robot designed in a bottom-up fashion could soldier on despite a damaged module and still might be able to complete some or all of its tasks.

Literally built from the bottom up
Cubelets toys allow kids to build robots by connecting stackable cubes. Each cube has some special part and code to control it.

HELLO, MY NAME IS:

Elmer and Elsie

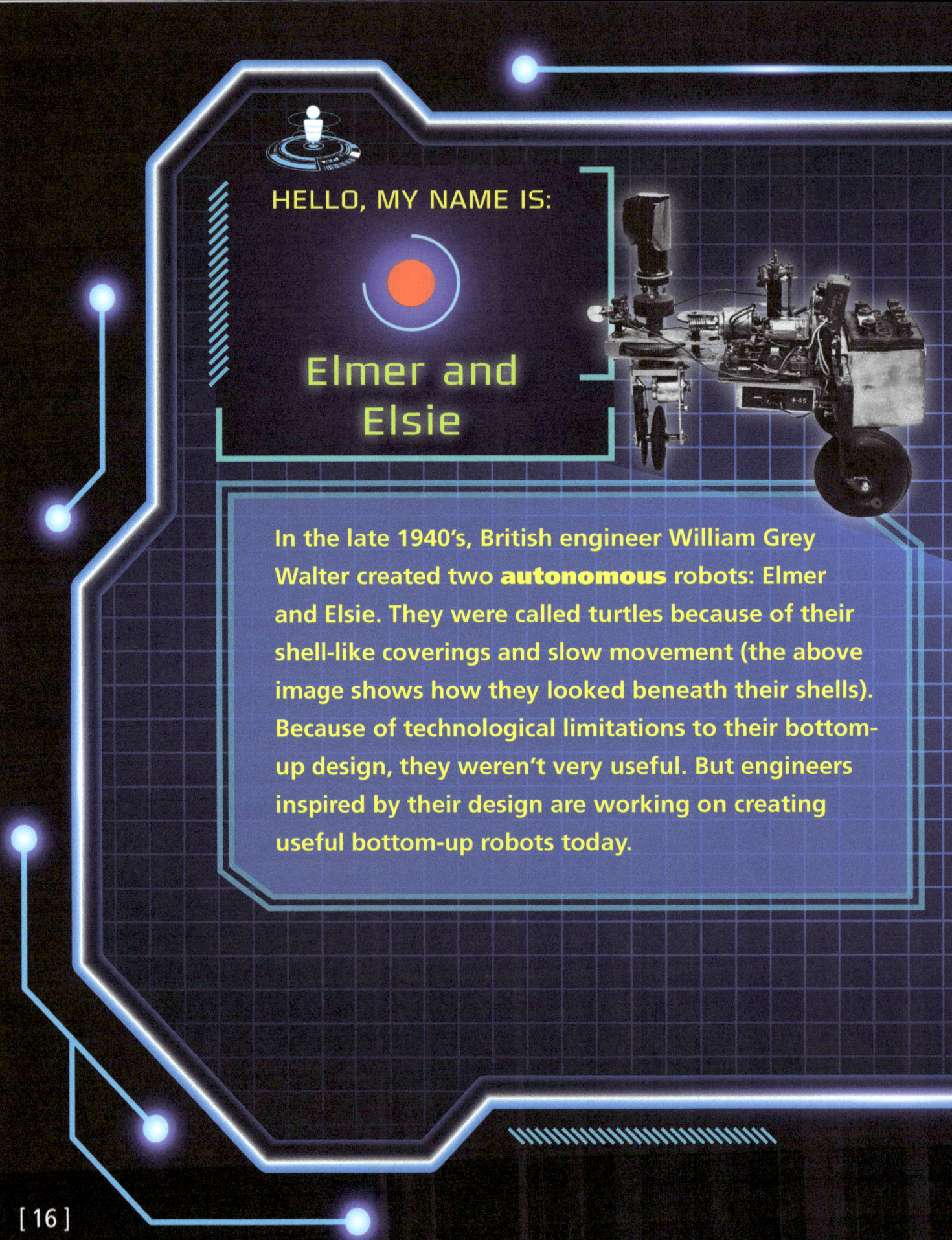

In the late 1940's, British engineer William Grey Walter created two **autonomous** robots: Elmer and Elsie. They were called turtles because of their shell-like coverings and slow movement (the above image shows how they looked beneath their shells). Because of technological limitations to their bottom-up design, they weren't very useful. But engineers inspired by their design are working on creating useful bottom-up robots today.

AUTONOMY
HIGH

Elmer and Elsie roamed around their enclosure, following light.

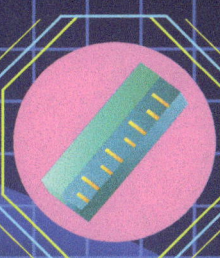

SIZE
10.5 inches (26.5 centimeters) long

WHAT'S IN A NAME?
Elmer stands for *El*ectro*m*echanical *R*obot. Elsie stands for *El*ectromechanical Robot, *L*ight *S*ensitive with *I*nternal and *E*xternal Stability.

MAKER
British engineer William Grey Walter

Uses of Bottom-Up Robotics

Because the bottom-up approach doesn't need much computing power, one of its most common uses is in toys. With a few simple rules, robotic pets can respond to sounds and touch, and imitate playfulness, fear, or excitement.

Bottom-up robotics can animate simple robotic toys, making them look far more intelligent than they really are.

Engineers probably won't create complex, **humanoid** robots using bottom-up robotics. But by following simple programs, swarms of simple mass-produced robots might clean plastic out of the ocean or pull weeds from fields. It wouldn't matter if some of them get stuck or break down because they would be so numerous and cheap. There could even be other robots that collect the damaged or stuck robots!

Swarm robotics uses at least some aspects of bottom-up robotics. In a swarm, many simple robots come together to perform more complex behavior.

Top-Down Robotics

In traditional **AI** robotics, a robot first senses the environment, makes a model of the environment in its computer, plans how to act based on its program and the model, and then performs the action. Unlike bottom-up architecture, this requires all parts of the robot to be directly connected. If one of the robot's **sensors** or **actuators** fails or if any of its code is corrupted or hacked, the robot will probably break down. But traditional robots make up for this in their ability to bring together many pieces of information and form plans, which bottom-up robots can't do.

Factories are perfect places for top-down robotics. On an assembly line, tasks are very well defined. For example, two parts might need to be put together, or small pieces might need sorting. But programmers must first figure out all the steps the robot will need to perform, and how it should respond to any variations.

Machine Learning

Machine learning is a field of **artificial intelligence** that programs computers and robots to learn from examples and from experience. Imagine if a self-driving car had to store millions of images of every street sign, car, rock, and pedestrian in order to identify them. It would need so much memory that there would be no room for passengers! A better way is to teach **software** how to categorize new objects as it goes.

Teaching computers and robots how to learn has been a goal of artificial intelligence researchers for a long time. They are making progress, but most machine learning is still pretty limited. People can learn different languages, how to drive a car, or how to bake. We can also figure out what we need to know. A robot might be able to learn to drive or play chess, but no robot comes close to the complexity of human learning.

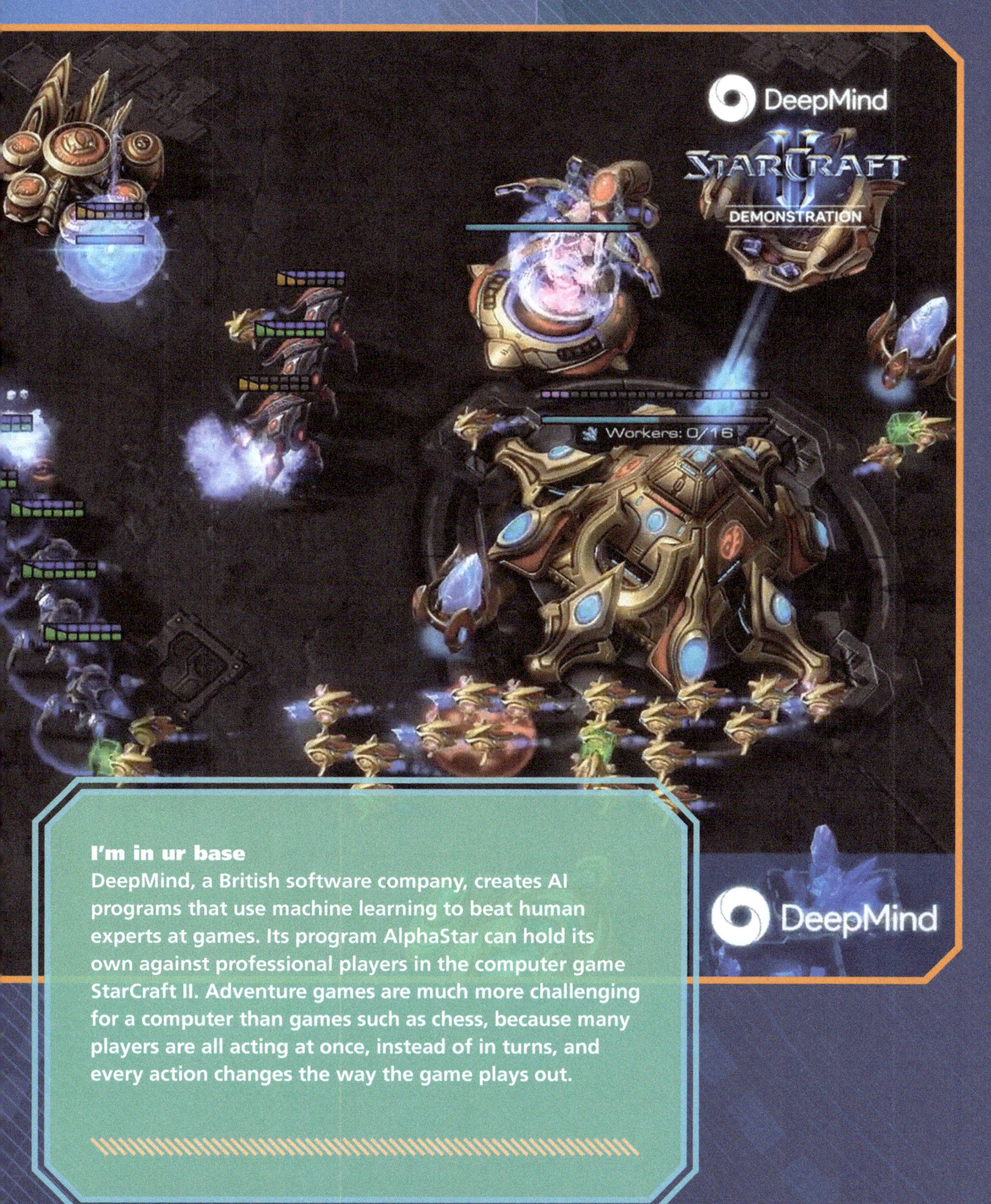

I'm in ur base

DeepMind, a British software company, creates AI programs that use machine learning to beat human experts at games. Its program AlphaStar can hold its own against professional players in the computer game StarCraft II. Adventure games are much more challenging for a computer than games such as chess, because many players are all acting at once, instead of in turns, and every action changes the way the game plays out.

Supervised Learning

There are two different types of **machine learning:** supervised and unsupervised. In supervised learning, humans know the right answers to the questions they are asking the **AI.** For instance, a self-driving car will have to recognize traffic signals and obey them. We know what a stop sign looks like and that cars are supposed to stop when they get to one.

Self-driving car **software** is trained through supervised learning. The program is shown many images of stop signs. It uses these data to figure out what makes a stop sign a stop sign. When it sees one on the street, it can then recognize it, even if it hasn't seen a picture of that particular stop sign before.

Are you a robot trainer?
Have you ever had to take a small test to prove you were a human before making an online purchase? You might have been training robots! The tech company Google started creating tests called reCAPTCHA's that involve spotting street signs and traffic signals in photographs. The responses are being used to train Waymo's self-driving cars. (Waymo and Google share the same parent company, Alphabet.) By tagging the signs, humans give the program examples to learn from.

Select all squares with street signs.
If there are none, click skip.

SKIP

Unsupervised Learning

In unsupervised learning, humans don't know the answers to the questions they are asking the **AI**. Unsupervised learning is much harder to design. But it has the potential to be even more useful than supervised learning because it doesn't need labeled training data.

In unsupervised learning, robots are instructed to look for patterns and develop their own methods to best accomplish their goals (such as avoiding collisions). For instance, if a self-driving car notices that more pedestrians cross a certain intersection every day at the same time, it might slow down near that intersection at that time even before it detects any people.

Driving isn't all stoplights and lane markers
Self-driving cars will have to anticipate and adjust to pedestrian behavior.

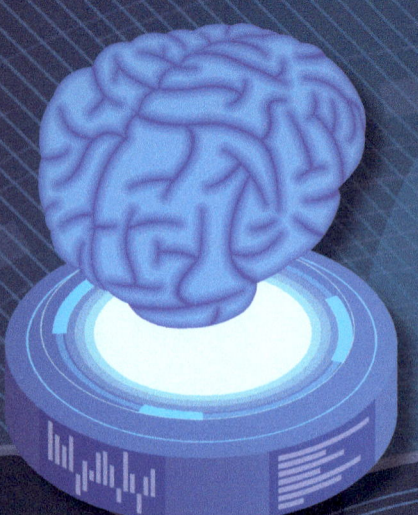

Learning Like Us: Neural Networks

Human brains are very different from computers. In a brain, rather than paths etched into silicon, living cells called neurons link together in a complex web. Signals flowing among these cells allow us to process

In one gripping experiment, a neural network was coupled with several robot arms. The neural network predicted how to grasp objects beneath the arms. An arm would try to grasp the object in the predicted way and then feed the result back into the neural network, leading to better predictions.

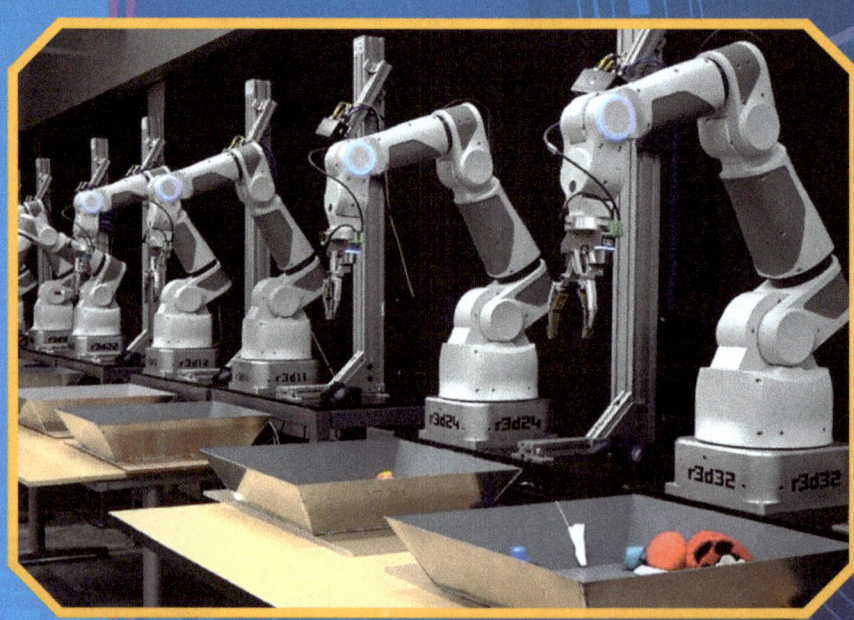

information coming in from our senses, think, and store memories. Computer programs called neural networks simulate how groups of neurons work to learn and solve problems. This method is also called deep learning.

Neural networks are trained in much the same way we are. They are shown labeled examples of an object or behavior. For example, a human could perform a task in virtual reality, showing the robot how to perform the same task with its **effectors.**

Neural networks have drawbacks, however. Computer **hardware** is not a brain, so a programmed neural network will be different from a living one. The human brain has about 100 billion neurons, with as many as 50 trillion connections between them. Neural networks cannot hope to match this complexity. But some AI researchers believe they are the most promising tool for humanlike robot learning.

"I've read this one already!" Scientists have used a neural network to train the research robot iCub to identify objects by trial and error, much the same way a child learns.

Learning from Demonstration

Industrial robots can be dangerous for people to be around when they are working. But a new breed of robots designed to work with humans, called **collaborative robots** or **cobots,** are making their way onto the factory floor. Many cobots not only work alongside workers but also need them in order to learn new tasks. A traditional industrial robot must go through a complicated programming process to learn a new task. But a worker can often train a cobot by moving its **effectors** through the task by hand. Once a worker has guided a cobot through the new task, the cobot remembers it and can repeat it.

The cobot LBR IIWA can be taught how to perform a task by a human operator. The operator can use a tablet interface, as shown here, or guide the 'bot through the task by hand.

HELLO, MY NAME IS:

Spot

Spot is a robotic dog designed to work with people in all kinds of environments. It can climb stairs, inspect equipment, and record video. With an arm attachment, it can lift small objects or pull people to safety in emergencies. Spot can be controlled remotely or programmed to do tasks in factories or in public spaces. It can also be programmed with AI, to figure out solutions on its own.

AUTONOMY
MEDIUM

Spot can be controlled remotely or programmed to do tasks on its own.

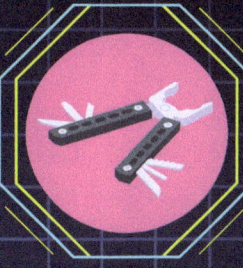
TRANSFORMER
Spot can be fitted with a variety of arms, cameras, carrying platforms, and sensors to help it do different jobs.

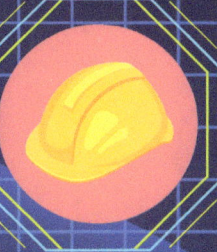
SAFETY
Spot is designed to work around people. It is often used to keep workers safe by taking on such hazardous tasks as machine inspections and bomb disposal. Spot's dog-shaped body is filled with sensors to help it avoid running into people or objects.

MAKER
Spot is made by Boston Dynamics.

[33]

Think about how much time people spend learning. Parents teach toddlers and children basic things about the world. Schools teach kids more advanced concepts. Universities teach adults details of complex subjects. Most people spend the first 20 years of their lives learning before they are ready to start a career.

Robotic learning is similarly taxing. Even if a robot learns 24 hours a day or learns faster than a person, it still takes time to train. Many kinds of **machine learning** also require large amounts of human effort. For example, in supervised learning, people have to provide labeled examples for the robots to learn from.

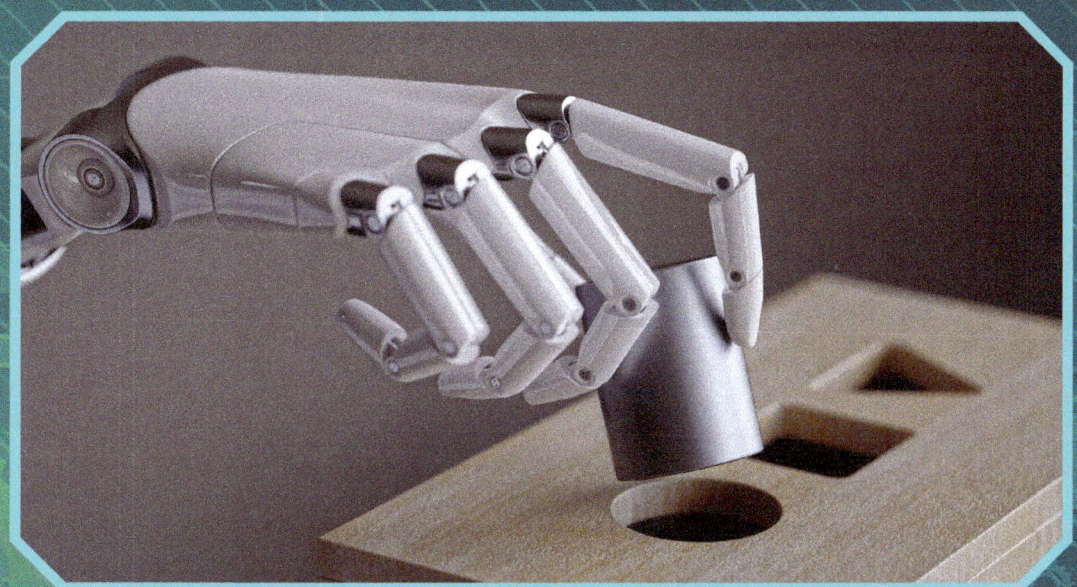

But machine learning has already changed how companies and researchers process data. Rather than creating robots that learn the exact same way we do, engineers are working to give robots just enough learning ability to improve the skills that robots already do well.

Learning Through Play

Playing is important work. When babies shake rattles or toddlers stack blocks, they are making connections that will help them as they grow. First, they are learning about their own bodies. They learn how their arms and fingers can move, how strong they are, and how best to hold things. They also learn about the objects themselves. They use this information to make predictions about how objects they see later will behave.

This is a powerful strategy for robots to use. A robot might start out with no knowledge of the properties of objects or how to perform tasks, but it could be programmed to learn them through moving itself around and manipulating objects. A robot that learns this way might be able to perform tasks even if something unexpected happens, such as another object getting in the way. It will have learned how to respond—such as by moving the object out of the way or working around it—by playing with similar objects.

Serious business
Babies, toddlers, and kids learn a lot from play. Robot researchers are hoping that robots could learn through play, too.

Learning Together

One great thing about humans is that when we discover something, we can let everyone else know. Imagine if our ancestors couldn't show each other which plants were poisonous or the best ways to hunt. We wouldn't have made it very far! Instead, we've set up whole institutions dedicated to the storing and spreading of knowledge (schools and libraries).

Most robots are not set up to learn from one another. If two **industrial robots** are working side-by-side and one successfully performs its task under unusual circumstances, it cannot tell its robot neighbor how it did it.

But this is starting to change. Programmers are networking robots of the same type together and programming them to share their experiences. Some research groups are even coming up with systems that let robots of all different kinds share knowledge with each other. Such shared learning could lead to a huge intelligence jump for all robots.

AIR-Cobot is a robot designed to inspect airplanes. Each AIR-Cobot is built to share its experiences over a network. Such sharing will make each inspection quicker and more thorough than the last, whether it takes place in Chicago or Beijing.

Robot Rights

Some people think that as robots get smarter, they might deserve to be given rights by governments, similar to humans. In 2022, an engineer working for tech company Google made headlines when he claimed that the company's AI program had achieved sentience—an awareness of self. Most experts dismissed his claim, pointing out that chatbots are good mimics. Imitating thought is not the same as thinking. But what if someday we decide that robots with AI are sentient? And how would we know?

Some people worry that if we give rights to AI robots, the companies that make the AI could avoid blame if the robots do something wrong. They think that the people who create intelligent robots should be responsible for any damages the robots might cause. They also point out that programmers are a long way from creating programs that even come close to human intelligence.

Citizen or spokesbot?
The robot Sophia has been granted citizenship in Saudi Arabia, but it is not clear exactly what that means. Some experts think it was a stunt to get attention for both the robot and the country.

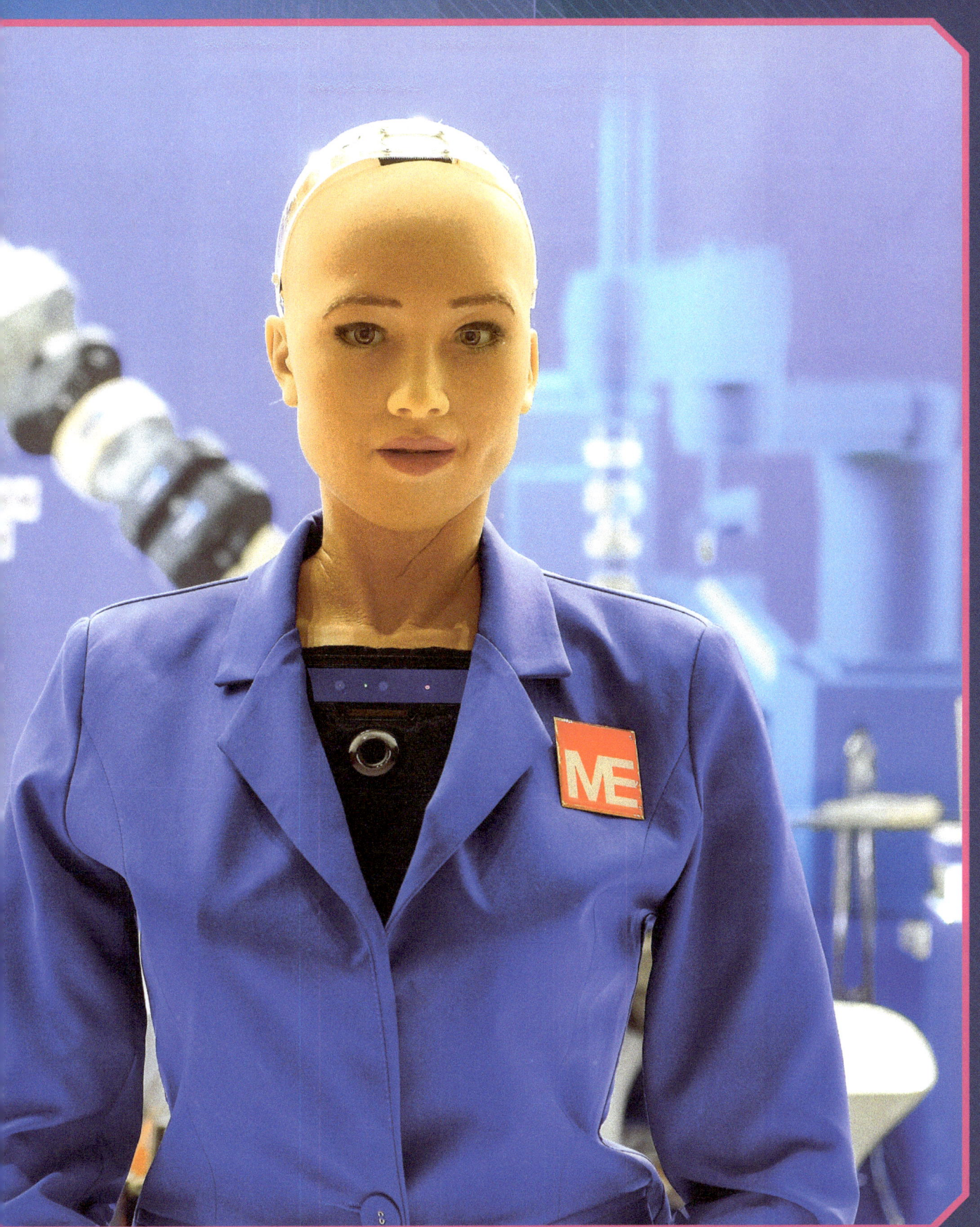

Robot Responsibilities

Before (if ever) robots have rights, they will also have responsibilities. Isaac Asimov, an American author, created what are called the Three Laws of Robotics as a device for his short stories. The laws deal with how intelligent robots behave towards people. First, a robot must not harm a human or allow a human to come to harm through inaction. Second, a robot must obey any order given to it by a human as long as it doesn't cause the robot to break the first law. Third, a robot must protect itself as long as doing so doesn't break the first two laws.

Although we are still a long way away from the superintelligent **humanoid** robots that Asimov wrote about, his Three Laws of Robotics have inspired people to think about how the law should treat robots. As smarter robots are created, they may have similar programming to keep them from harming people or themselves.

A self-driving car—and its programmers—must be responsible for protecting its passengers and the people around it.

Living with Smarter Robots

As robots get better at thinking and learning, they will become even more useful. A robotic housecleaner may learn where to put the dishes, or a self-driving delivery truck might figure out when a household is likely to be running low on bread and drive over with a fresh loaf.

Will robots become too useful? Some people worry about the effects of **automation** on employment. **Industrial robots** have been replacing people in factories for more than 50 years. Researchers estimate that each industrial robot replaces about three human workers on average in the United States—though there are new jobs building and programming robots. **AI**-equipped robots and computers may be able to do many more jobs in the future. As robots do more work, governments may act to ensure everyone benefits, by reducing the work week or providing every citizen with a basic income.

Robo-Picasso
Robots and AI programs can play music, write stories, and paint pictures, such as this one from a robot called Cloudpainter. They might someday be as creative as people. But will we enjoy art created by robots in the same way? Or is the joy in being a human, making art?

Hands-On Robotics

Want to get started making robots? Jump right in!

Get Coding

However cool a robot's body looks, a robot's most important part is its brainy **software**—the clever programming that controls how it moves, acts, and thinks. That means one of the best ways to get started in robotics is by learning to code. Where to begin? Anywhere! You don't even need a robot.

Scratch

Many kids start with a visual block-based program such as Scratch, available for free online at scratch.mit.edu. You can use it to make computer games or program robots.

Python

Python is a versatile programming language that is often the first written coding language that programmers learn. There are many online sites where you can learn and practice, including Khan Academy, Udemy, Codecademy, Kids Python, Girls Who Code, and many others.

Coding brains
A robot's brain is a computer. Programs control everything the robot does. A great robot starts with an elegant program to run it.

 **C++**
Once you've mastered the basics, C++ is a more advanced programming language that will let you program all kinds of robots.

There are many more programming languages out there. Which language you decide to use depends on what you want your robot to do. But once you learn one, learning others is easier.

Also check out:
- Coding camps—look online or in your community
- Code clubs—are often also interested in robotics
- Hour of Code (code.org)
- USA Coding Olympiad (USACO)
- Informatics Olympiad (International)

Or ask at your local school, library, or maker space.

Glossary

actuator a device, such as a motor, that provides movement to a robot.

android a type of humanoid robot designed to look as humanlike as possible.

artificial intelligence (AI) the ability of a computer system to process information in a manner similar to human thought or to exhibit humanlike behavior.

automation the use of machines to perform tasks that require decision making.

autonomy the degree to which a robot can make decisions without input from a human operator to achieve a goal.

collaborative robot (cobot) an industrial robot designed to work closely with people and share workspaces with them.

effector the part of the robot's body, such as a wheel or a gripper, that is moved by an actuator and interacts with the environment to perform an action.

hardware the physical parts of a computer.

humanoid shaped like or resembling a human.

industrial robot a robot that works in a factory to help create a product.

machine learning a field of artificial intelligence that involves computer programs learning from examples and from experience.

sensor a device that takes in information from the outside world and translates it into code.

software a general term for computer programs. A computer program is mostly made up of a sequence of instructions. The instructions tell a computer what to do and how to do it.

structured environment in robotics, an area in which a robot operates that has been specially designed to reduce the number of unexpected occurrences while the robot is working. The flow of people, vehicles, and items not involved in the robot's task is usually restricted.

unstructured environment in robotics, an area in which a robot operates that has not been specially designed for it. People, vehicles, and other things may pass through the area in which the robot works.

Index

A
actuators, 8, 20
AIR-Cobot, 38-39
AlphaStar (program), 23
androids, 40-41
artificial intelligence (AI), 8, 12-13, 22, 40, 44; bottom-up approach, 14-19; top-down approach, 20-21. See also machine learning
Asimov, Isaac, 42
assembly lines, 20-21
automation, 44
autonomy, 10-11, 17, 33

B
Boston Dynamics (company), 33
brains, 8-9; human, 28-29; insect, 14

C
cars, self-driving, 22, 24, 26-27, 42-43
cobots, 30-31, 38-39
coding, 46-47
computers, 8, 20, 28-29
Cubelets (toys), 15

D
deep learning, 29
DeepMind (company), 23

E
effectors, 8, 29, 30
Elmer and Elsie (robots), 16-17
emergent behavior, 15
employment, 44-45

F
facial recognition, 12-13

G
games, 23
Genghis (robot), 14
Google Inc., 24, 40

H
hardware, 8-9, 29
humanoid robots, 19, 42

I
iCub (robot), 29
industrial robots, 6, 10-11, 20-21, 38-39, 44. See also cobots
insects, 14
intelligence, 6-7

L
lawn mowers, robotic, 6-7
LBR IIWA (robot), 30-31
learning, human, 4, 22, 26, 28-29, 35-37

M
machine learning, 22-23; difficulty with, 34-35; from demonstration, 30-31; networked units, 38-39; neural networking in, 28-29; supervised, 24-25, 35; through play, 36-37; unsupervised, 26-27. See also artificial intelligence (AI)

N
neural networks, 28-29

P
play, 36-37

R
reCAPTCHA's, 24-25
robots, thinking and learning by, 4-11; employment and, 44-45; rights and responsibilities with, 40-43. See also artificial intelligence (AI); machine learning

S
safety, 30, 33, 42-43
Saudi Arabia, 40
sense-plan-act, 8
sensors, 8, 20
software, 8, 22, 24
Spot (robot), 32-33
Sophia (robot), 8-9, 40-41
StarCraft II (game), 23
structured environments, 4, 10-11
swarm robotics, 19

T
Three Laws of Robotics, 42
toys, 15, 18
turtles (robots), 16-17

U
unstructured environments, 5, 8, 10, 42

W
Walter, William Grey, 16-17
Waymo (company), 24

www.ingramcontent.com/pod-product-compliance
Lightning Source LLC
Chambersburg PA
CBHW061254170426
43191CB00041B/2422